POETIC REVELATIONS of
Eternal Life

Bob McCluskey

POETIC REVELATIONS OF ETERNAL LIFE
Copyright © 2016 by Bob McCluskey

All rights reserved. Neither this publication nor any part of this publication may be reproduced or transmitted in any form or by any means, electronic or mechanical, including photocopying, recording or any information storage and retrieval system, without permission in writing from the author.

Thanks to Sunshine Hills Foursquare Church (6749 120th Street, Delta, BC V4E 2A7, Phone 604-594-0810, Fax 604-594-6673) for all of their help and support with my books.

Printed in Canada

ISBN: 978-1-4866-1108-9

Word Alive Press
131 Cordite Road, Winnipeg, MB R3W 1S1
www.wordalivepress.ca

Cataloguing in Publication may be obtained through Library and Archives Canada

DEDICATION

As the years go by, I am pleasantly surprised to find that time and again, when the well seems to have finally dried up, some unexpected inspiration pops into my head and away we go again. I am very thankful to God for resurgent inspiration and continue to find great edification in writing poetry.

Some critics might suggest that attributing this poetic inspiration to God would be too much of a stretch since surely God would do much better than that...Be that as it may, I will continue to dedicate my poetry to God and just keep pounding the keys as inspiration comes, maybe it's a pride thing Eh! Common sense would dictate that this, my tenth book of poetry is probably my last due to age (90) and increasing infirmity but that's in God's hands.....Sayonara!

SECTION ONE

SILENT WINTER SCREAM
September 6, 2014

Out of the nether world unseen
assassins lurk.
To ravage lovely summer's green
as helpless flowers silent scream,
reveals their hurt.

Their loveliness rewarded so,
doth seem unfair.
As season's unrelenting flow,
delivers a descending blow
from frigid air.

But out of death doth life ensue
in garden's blight.
The old must die to thus renew,
God's garden wide, from just a few
who lost the fight.

So doth the wheel of life revolve
unceasingly.
Our intellect doth never solve
the mystery of Jesus call,
man's good deeds, sin doth ne'er absolve.
The only hope for man, must be
when he commits to Jesus Christ
eternally.

AH, THE JEW
Aug. 1, 2015

Ah, the Jew,
disdained, profaned, yet by God pre-ordained
to be chosen.
Defiant, uncompliant, yet in the end reliant
on God's declaration, throughout time indelibly
frozen.

Ah, the Jew,
by every nation in the world as time unfurled,
    rejected.
But all that toucheth Israel,
    shall taste God's unexpected
ire gainst the hatred in their hearts,
    Satanically directed
gainst the Jew, the apple of God's eye.

Ah, the Jew,
one day will see Messiah
    who they blindly spurned
two thousand years ago, and now returned
as Jesus hath proclaimed he would...
    Lo, I come,
and will dwell in the midst of Israel,
    for everyone.

Ah, the Jew,
with them we believers now wait,
    with a fervent hope
whilst the scoffers fill ever with hate.
But Jerusalem shall descend,
    as God didst intend,
twelve whole pearls designating each gate.

TIMED CONDITIONING
September 1, 2014

Why do good people do bad things
Which they would not usually do
What element is it that brings
Evil out from the heart of me and you

A prime example, of course
Is the Germans in world war two
What they did to the Jews is worse
Than anything we might construe

We might think we're above all that
But if we were thrust in their place
We too would obey our commands every day
With an innocent look on our face

It does not come on sudden you know
Timed conditioning plays a big part
We would go to places we're told to go
But that is only the start

Propaganda machines then crank out
Their mass marketing works of deceit
Fill our hearts with hate to seal their fate
With a blood lust to turn up the heat

Then the final determining factor
One uniform's just like the rest
To become a most common reactor
Anonymity says it best

So we'd better beware who's elected
We do have a Prime Minister who
Unselfishly renders Israel support
As the Bible commands us to

A new war seems to be in the offing
And our enemy's acts seem obscener
Will we stoop to their level and act like the Devil
Or stand strong with a righteous demeanour

ARRUNJELAY
August 28, 2014

A stranger wandered close within
The confines of a country inn
How strange his visage didst appear
No one dared venture close to hear
His fetid breath proclaim, Arrunjelay!

Finishing off his watery soup
Then standing, scarce above a stoop
He hobbled grunting, thru the door
Whilst tripping o'er the threshold, swore
Casting anger to the night, Arrunjelay!

His threadbare rags would scarce suffice
To body warmth retain, entice
Men sitting warm before the fire
To open door, expressed their ire
As windswept voice flung back, Arrunjelay!

The darkened street held no remorse
From driving snow's unyielding course
Succumbing to exhaustion's test
A snow bank beckoned him to rest
He mumbled as he closed his eyes, Arrunjelay!

They found him in the morning there
A frozen corpse with vacant stare
And clutched within his cold embrace
A paper white without a trace of message
Just one word's emblazoned glare, Arrunjelay!

They searched his pockets just to see
If some clue might explain his mystery
They found a tiny bible there
With his name inscribed with greatest care
And underneath in bold display...Arrunjelay!

WE ALL ARE ONE
August 18, 2014

I hear the cry for unity,
"We All Are One!"
And in a way we truly be
beyond our gross disunity,
from one source sprung.

But are we one in Spirit
from our hearts?
I do see great disparity
betwixt so many folk and me,
as peace departs.

The word of God declares
that God loves everyone.
It does not say
in any way,
we're all God's son.

The Bible says that Jesus is
God's Only Begotten Son.
We who become
joint heirs with Christ,
become adopted sons.

This choice in life, each man
is called upon to make.
From Adam we didst all arise,
our second Adam, Jesus Christ,
will not thee forsake.

So yes, from common source
In God we've all begun.
But some will not Christ Jesus see,
the great division comes when we,
and Christ are one.

FROM THY GLORY
August 17, 2014

Ah love, in its transitory
Emblazure of passion intense
Why must love fade
From thy sweet adulade
From thy glory

Why must first loving encounter
Become a diminishing story
From love's moment of birth
With its laughter and mirth
From thy glory

From whence doth consuming fire
Vacillate ever before me
Doth the cares of my day
Steal the essence away
From thy glory

Such concentrate of adulation
So fabled in song and history
Must not ever decay
Nor steal essence away
From thy glory

When I stand before Jesus I'll know
If transubstantiation's allegory
If it is, God will show
No device from below
Can e'er lessen the glow
From His glory

HOW MANY SOULS
August 14, 2014

How many souls have passed
Through this vain life
Each in his turn, importantly
For art we then not rife
With life beyond rude measure
In our urgency

Whilst yet our years
Display not numbers over large
Doth this apply to we
Whom latterly our time
Comsumeth time so hungrily
As importunely, time yet disappears

Self awareness doth consume
The very young indeed
Whilst we who stoopeth
Under weight of years
Are thus decreed
To see reality revealed

And thus, diminishing
In self importance now
Our inner eye doth see
With increased clarity
Life's indiscernible disparity
From all encompassing eternity

And so, as each in turn
Doth slowly slide from sight
Wherever then will we again
Recover in encroaching night
The destiny of all in whom
We once didst so delight

INSIDE
September 4, 2014

Man's blackness ruleth inside.
Not the skin, but what's within
where ugly passions hide
inside.

That's where they hide, inside.
While outer visage fashions peace,
within, man's hatred finds release,
inside.

Inside, where stomach acids churn,
while outwardly compassions yearn
for circumstance to stress adjourn,
inside.

Peace! Peace! We hear man's outward cry,
whilst deep within where blackness rules,
we act like aggravated fools,
inside.

Without the Christ, the man of peace
to cleanse us of our pride.
That turmoil will not ever cease,
inside.

TRUE PEACE
August 9, 2014

Where doth peace reside without the mind of man
and the Spirit of God to formulate peace.
Peace fleeth from unrestrained emotions
unharnessed, rampant, filled with unspoken,
undefined satisfactions.
When man turns from selfishness to introspection,
to honest examination of unrestrained anger,
He discovers his baser self lying hidden deep inside,
waiting to be fed some real or misunderstood affront
and to be then unleashed in an unrestrained explosion
of offended anger.
If man would but subscribe to and fulfill Christ's
commandment to love one another as He has loved us,
we would then turn the other cheek, love those who
hate us and pray for those who despitefully use us,
to the glory of God the Father.
Would that this could be but alas, to achieve that level
of Christ's love while sojourning in sinful flesh would
be for me personally, and without doubt for you also,
next to impossible.
This brings us to the inescapable conclusion that
    true peace
will not come to mankind until Christ returns to
    banish sin
and to establish His eternal Kingdom here on earth,
even so, come Lord Jesus.

WE HAVE TO HAVE FOOD
August 2, 2014

Seven billion's the world population,
and they have to be fed every day.
Without sounding too crass,
they cannot just eat grass,
or like cows, repast daily on hay.

It don't work that way when you're hungry,
you know what we mean, you've been there.
You just have to have food,
we don't mean to sound rude,
but it could be a bloody affair.

Up to now, it's one house that we're talking,
what if the whole country's that way.
All the crops in the field
had a terrible yield,
and the stores are quite empty today.

Oh, the rest of the world will come calling,
to supply all the food that we need.
But what if the famine
has hit the whole world,
leaving nothing on which we might feed.

You might say that this never could happen,
drought or flooding has happened before.
The good book does explain
when God held back the rain,
or earth's fountains surged over the shore.
So we'd better acknowledge God's blessings,
each committing to Jesus, God's Son.
If God caused a great drought,
'twould not leave many out,
to populate in the ages to come.

GOLD IS A TERRIBLE GOAD
July 24, 2014

El Dorado, the mythical city of gold
for centuries drew man's heart.
In the minds of men it exists of old,
and has for thousands of years I'm told,
the result of greed from the start.

Some men have immunity, they say,
its established at birth in their genes.
To live out their lives in a simpler way,
to just work for their families every day,
they've learned what faithfulness means.

Gold doth of course with innocence lie,
it holdeth no conscience within.
It's the love of gold that is evil's source,
some men have gold but do share of course,
letting love of Jesus begin.

But most seeking gold are a driven lot,
they will get it at any price.
Through a needles eye, could a camel go,
ere a rich man might come into heaven, I know,
but some rich men avoided that vice.

Usually greed will succeed in the end,
piling up a large fortune grand.
Gold meaneth more than the hand of a friend,
friendships and avarice can't seem to blend,
for these masters of all they command.

At the end of the road, gold's a terrible goad
that propels to the great divide.
They'd determine their end if they'd only contend
with the choice of Jesus to be their friend,
for them too, He was crucified.

RICHES MOCK
July 24, 2014

What thoughts ingratiate a mind
From whence doth affirmation come
Can man yet seek God's heavens far
Though blind

Will man's denial satisfy ineptitude
For those three score and ten encumbered years
Of stumbling blindly thru a lifetime to conclude
With man's worst fears

None so blind as those with eyes who see not
None so deaf as those who will not hear
Denying truth, they travel thru life fear fraught
While they're here

And well might man envision fear of endless night
When Light of all the world doth light exterminate
Accumulated riches mock, when end in sight
Doth terminate

WAR BETWEEN EVIL AND GOOD
July 18, 2014

Let's face it, a war between evil and good
surrounds us if we would but see.
We do see it in Scripture, the picture's quite clear,
but that's rather detached, evil lurks very near,
in fact within you, within me.

This war rages on in the heart of us all,
but out of sight deep within.
With his mind, man is serving the laws of his Gods,
while his flesh appetizes for sin.
For the good he would do, he finds he does not,
Evil then, man instinctively lauds.

God did make a way to His Heaven for us,
but if we don't know Christ, we won't care.
Without Jesus we're deaf and most certainly blind,
as we look at the world thru an obdurate mind,
of this war, are we even aware.

So Christ is the key and if ever we,
Will acknowledge our sin and confess.
We will find that the blinkers remove from our eyes,
we will joyfully yield to His loving surprise,
we'll see clearly through Satan's unyielding disguise,
freed at last, from the body of this death.

ITS NOT ALL ABOUT ME
July 10, 2014

I was watching a Roman Catholic lawyer,
    not a Nun, a Sister,
who founded and heads a ministry
that seeks to bring
a fairness in this world to everyone, in everything.

Now, I could go on about her work,
    her even-handedness.
But she revealed something in me that
    opened up my eyes to see
a truth I will expand to thee,
    my own self-centeredness.

The areas of deepest care,
    the objects of my fervent prayer ,
I bring before the Lord and focus very hard,
    forsooth,
but ever centered just on me and mine
    and that's the truth.

I realize now my selfishness and recognise my sin.
I must look very far afield and welcome others in,
like those I know who suffer so, today I will begin.

Forgive me Lord, I now repent and
    take to heart this heaven sent
reminder of my selfishness,
    the Middle East under duress.
Lord, save I pray the innocent
    who suffer heaviness.

I've taken this command to heart and
    purpose this is just a start,
the needs I have God knoweth,
    so I have no need to tell.
I'll leave them in His tender care and
    pray for others everywhere
as well.

DOTH MEMORY CONTRIBUTE
July 5, 2014

Doth memory contribute ought to life
as curtain lowers gradually.
Or doth it bring to man such drab device,
to mind naught but remembrance of tragedy.

Or doth memory on the other hand devise,
as sunset falls and dark of night doth grow.
To savor only fond remembrance live,
as death contrives to rise up from below.

Cold moon that shineth on a world at rest,
indifferent to life tragically deposed.
Losing energies and favor that once blest
with optimisms energetic goad.

As weakness rules and legs refuse to ramble,
as leisure beckons with imprisoning power.
Those chores of old take far too long to handle,
where minutes reigned, requireth now one hour.

In memory idly room to room, to search love
of friends and lovers who have disappeared.
Forgetting who we entered there in search of,
with sudden memory loss, contrition seared.

But now this tale doth end upon a true note,
as darkness settleth in and death subscribes.
For Christ hath conquered death!
Behold, a true quote.
In your wisdom, embrace Christ, ere life subsides.

WAR OF AGES
July 3, 2014

The stage is set, the heavens gathered in grand array,
to view the wonder of all creation on display.
The woman Israel, deigned by God in all the earth
to be the vessel God availeth to bring to birth
the Christ of God.

Then another wonder, a great red dragon
    in heaven appeared,
with his tail, a third of heavens angels
    who greatly feared
were cast by the dragon all the way down to earth,
where the dragon didst wait to devour
    when Israel gave birth
to God.

The woman brought forth a Man Child,
    resplendent in glory,
who would rule all the heavens and
    all God's creation, for He
was the Son of God who would
    rule with a rod of iron,
the only One whom all heaven and earth
    could truly rely on
to exist.

For Christ is before all things and by Him
 all things are,
He then removed to the throne of God
 in heaven far.
The woman Israel hath a wilderness place
 prepared in God's light,
to be fed a thousand two hundred and
 threescore days, to hide
in plain sight.

And there was war in heaven, Michael and
 his angels fought,
the dragon and his angels were defeated and
 prevailed not.
They were cast down to the earth where they
 ever bring great woe
against all mankind where they have become
 an implacable foe
of both man and God.

The dragon doth now war with Israel's physical/
 spiritual seed,
to bring sin and destruction on earth and
 destroy man's need
of a Savior to remedy all with His pristine,
 cleansing blood.
Christ shall soon bind Satan and his angels
 in a final, consuming flood
of righteous wrath.

THE FOLK I HAVE KNOWN
July 1, 2014

The folk I've known from almost ninety years,
and over the first half without the Lord.
We sinned together ignorant of fears,
indulging lust, indifferent of reward.

They come into our lives without a plan,
to stay awhile, perhaps a longer time.
But ultimately leave us, to a man,
tho for a while, they be a pal o' mine.

Where are they now, be some as yet alive,
I pray they be and have the gift of God.
I shudder at the loss they wouldst derive,
if with eternal death they now be shod.

Oh God, how great the gift thou hast bestowed,
on those whose hearts with Holy Spirit thrive.
Whose countenance with joy delightful glowed,
to be with Thee, eternally alive.

So many we indulged with friendship grand,
O'er those first fifty years in ignorance.
As hourglass displayeth trickling sand,
just so, for memory we look askance.

But God alone doth make the final choice,
mere man doth merit naught but to obey.
Mans destiny's regret or great rejoice,
thou wouldst do well to choose the Lord today.

PASSIONS IN MEN
June 29, 2014

The passions in men that Satan doth bait,
so intense they defy revelation.
Lying hidden, to manifest deep inside,
lusting after their love of infanticide,
or some other extreme deviation.

Or men, lusting after the bodies of men,
to perform their abomination.
Defying tradition by flouting their lust,
indifferent to men who they now can trust
to accept their aberration.

Sin favors darkness to prosper unseen,
abominating all righteousness.
To lust after children's bodies for sex,
what lust of the flesh might they generate next
to deceive but to never confess.

But God is not mocked, there's a price to be paid,
either here or the judgement to come.
Men now call good evil and call evil good,
just as the Bible revealed that they would,
but God's judgement's for everyone.

Just as God's Salvation is also for all,
that is, all who will bow the knee
to the Savior Lord Jesus while we still live,
death is not the end, for the truth of it is,
we will live for eternity.

I WANDERED BY THE SHORE
June 18, 2014

I wandered by the shore one dreamy morn,
the sea was calm, as was my soul within.
The breathless air, of angriness was shorn,
as hearts rejoiced in life at day's begin.

Along the gravelled shore, there vaguely came
a ghostly form, emerging from the mist.
His gait betrayed a hindrance, he was lame,
the stones and driftwood, progress didst resist.

At his slow but sure approachment I observed,
his easy balance, confidence revealed.
From the unexpected, he was not unnerved,
to my curiosity, his peculiarity appealed.
A blessed day this morning sir, I bid thee,
as I spoke, his searching gaze observed my slog.
He answered not a word as yet, but bid me
with gallant gesture, to be seated on a log.

The shore, littered with logging's vagrant drifters,
did each in silence, proffer us a seat.
The sand that occupied our shoes as sifters,
necessitated shoe removal from our feet.

Good Sir, what brings thee early to this strand,
after careful attendance to amenities, I asked.
His answer didst surprise, he took my hand
to answer in a courtly manner, life has tasked

each one of us with earthly labors to attend,
for life is hard, as vagrant lumberings I seek.
Through rains and windswept wanderings I wend,
though age and rank infirmity hath left me weak.

Each candidate for salvage, I with pinch bar roll
to water's edge, preparing it for tow.
I have a beat up salvage boat, age has taken toll,
how it floateth through each day, I'll never know.

Since time hangs loosely on you now, I'll bend your ear,
for you have showed desire to peer within.
My history I'll share with you, although quite drear,
this log is hard on my retard, painfully quite thin.

The vagaries of life exact a heavy price betimes,
I once was vaulted high in man's esteem.
A sudden change in fortune and some heavy fines,
reduced me of my family and home, to this demean.

Men came to savor wisdom, laved with great aplomb,
a university professor, mine employ.
Men's worship and respect was what I craved alone,
and for many years enthroned, I didst enjoy.

But fortune faltered as gross shame engulfed
    my life,
my friends and family cast me then aside.
Of the pills I had to swallow, the bitterest was
    my wife,
whom I loved most dear, since she became my bride.

And so you see me now bereft, of all that life
    didst bless,
but with heart free of remorse, Christ let me in.
Which is best, the world or my salvation, you assess,
please choose wisely, ask the Lord to cleanse your sin.

With that, the kindly stranger stood despite the pain,
then with courtly bow, he bid a grand adieu.
Blithely sauntered down the beach despite the rain,
and left me with my faith in sad review.

I watched him disappear into the mist,
    a gentle wraith,
and wondered, was that person really real.
Or did God dispatch an angel to encourage
    my weak faith,
my salvation now, displayed a new appeal.

BASE ATTITUDES
June 25, 2014

About the world, as war on war doth rage,
as man's desire to hate comsumeth life.
Man crawls into this many festered age
of melancholy, laced with ardent strife.

To manifest a plethora of same
addiction, to base attitudes of heart.
Base attitudes, by any other name
wouldst yet devise to render man apart.

And is it then for this, that Jesus died
as love flowed hot and bloody from the cross.
When Jesus Holiness was crucified
in stark array, didst Satan suffer loss.

For Jesus took the keys to death and hell,
now death forever more hath lost its sting.
Yet sin most onerous doth yet foretell,
rebellious man's eternal suffering.

Rebellion is the key to man's demise,
refusing to obey Christ's clarion call.
But time departeth, destiny doth rise,
to final curtain's inexorable fall.

WITH BLINDED EYE
June 16, 2014

There seem as many opinions
As men, to believe the Devil's lie
They're not afraid, of the choices they made
Approaching the ever encroaching parade
To die

And this may be true, perhaps of you
As it is of me, without fail
But I hold no fear, for the One I endear
As my last breath with conscience clear
I exhale, awaits

But I wonder how, as the end draws nigh
Deep in their hearts, do they look to the sky
Is their spirit man struggling strong to awake
Their conscience from choices wrong, they make
With blinded eye

2 Peter 3:9
The Lord is not slack concerning His promise,
as some men count slackness;
but is longsuffering to us-ward,
not willing that any should perish,
but that all should come to repentance.

WHEN HEAVENS PARTED
June 9, 2014

What is a life, does it depend
on paths we wend, or prime location.
On riches earned, on challenge spurned,
so unconcerned, no consternation.

Must then there be for you, for me,
man's infamy, man's admiration.
Will we explore life's mystery,
not just accept, blind limitation.

I pose these thoughts to you my friend,
as you reflect on life's duration.
Sometimes you lost, there was a cost,
tho some events, brought grand elation.

But as the end, comes nearer now,
where does importance, really lie.
As values seem to change somehow,
what matters now, is how we die.

May I impart, a truth revealed
when heavens parted, many splendored.
God filled my heart, my future sealed
by Jesus Christ, when I surrendered.

OPERATION OVERLORD
June 6, 2014

June 6, 2014, marks seventy years
Since allied forces stormed Normandy's beach
A vast armada of warships grand
From England to France didst almost reach
To cover the channel from land to land
Men's blood would soak up Normandy's sand
But God knew

Men by their thousands went storming ashore
Through waters covered in floating dead
For most, a baptism of glorious war
This was after all, what war was for
As the ocean was turning red
Thousands of spirits of men were released
But God knew

With their craft approaching that enemy hell
Were men's minds occupied by prayer
They would have no illusions of what related
In Normandy's savagery, were they fated
To die, what destiny there awaited
As they steeled themselves, who could tell
But God knew

OPERATION OVERLORD, the invasion was named
And aptly so, one might say
This particular war was on Hitler blamed
But many other historic wars remained
With plenty of blame to go around
Since Satan has had his day
But God knew

Where are their spirits now, every boy
May each one be eternally saved
May their souls be redeemed by the
    prayers they prayed
In the moments before their lives were stayed
As they answered the call, evil must be destroyed
Not knowing the forces of hell, deployed
But God knew

NO WORLDLY GUARANTEES
May 31, 2014

I lay in bed supine one morning,
    with my linen snood adorning,
as my mind swam upward from below.
With retirement in the making,
    I was resolutely taking
my sweet time, with nowhere imminent to go.

A troubling thought gave me a fright
    as I awakened from the night,
of last night's news report, folks on the run.
Who would mind their own affair,
    when unbidden from the air
bombs would fall, and blow their
    homes to kingdom come.

Rudely wakened from their slumbers,
    in untold but frantic numbers,
becoming refugees to flee into the night.
Abandoned in their tracks,
    with just the clothing on their backs,
seeking safety with no rescuing in sight.

Not just the young and strong,
    the old and feeble came along,
they had to come, with nowhere else to stay.

I tried to think if it was me,
>	with my sore and gimpy knee
and my racking cough that wouldn't go away.

Great thanksgiving thoughts welled up,
>	about my overflowing cup,
I wondered how I'd fare if I must flee.
I thought how tenuous the world,
>	when seeming comfort is unfurled
with no more pension, no more anything for free.

How would we ever get along
>	amidst some teeming hungry throng,
not knowing where our food was coming from.
We have food, a bed, a home,
>	from our birth until we're grown,
but we have no guarantee distress won't come.

I know the only guarantee,
>	I hope for you, it is for me,
is the absolute assurance I receive
from instruction that is given
>	in the Bible truths for livin',
all you do is accept Jesus and believe.

MAN'S NOTORIOUS DISDAIN
June 4, 2014

Casual, my glance o'er garden lying by
Doth no vantage gain
God's creation manifested glorious
To this crass unappreciative eye
Never lessening man's notorious
Disdain

Why doth God design such radiant beauty
Often to be cast abroad unseen
Surely not from pity or from duty
While man doth with indifference, demean
Rather, God doth lavish in perpetuity
Man's searching dream

Had we only eyes to see God's gifting
Indiscriminately spread o'er man's domain
To raise our eyes above would be uplifting
As God from chaff, His precious wheat be sifting
To salvage from hell-fire's eternal flame
Repentant man

ITS UP TO YOU
May 12, 2014

To face a sword
What then, reward
Or arrow true
The end of you
To face a gun
No place to run
Oncoming tank
The world goes blank
What you pursue
And have to do
Determines what
Becomes of you

It all depends
On you my friends
The lives you live
The love you give
The choice you make
The heart you break
Could well be yours
Salvation's heart
Alone will start
If you choose Christ
While you're alive
You will survive

GOD'S GOODNESS AND SEVERITY
May 17, 2014

The strident voice of those self righteously
Decrying in man's wisdom, if a God doth live
And yet permit the sad destruct of little ones
Who have not sinned, who no offences give
I cannot worship Him

They stand in moral judgement of almighty God
Innocuous as fly specks on earth's cringing face
Seeking not Divine approval, only men's applaud
Without repentance, will ingest eternity's disgrace
No heaven ever will invite them in

In divine humility, God doth deign to answer thus
Though in the larger scheme of things, need not
In Romans 11:22, King James conjecture sings
In God's goodness and severity, man is never taught
To sin

To them which fell, severity, but unto thee, goodness
But only if thy continuing in goodness, doth manifest
Otherwise, thou wilt no doubt,
    encounter no God goodness
Thy fate wilt then depend on you, to pass the test
May repentance now begin

With blinding scales upon their eyes,
    they succumb to Satan's lies
Without the will or inclination then to look
At the evidence presented
    which lost men always despise
The sacred revelation in the Bible,
    God's most blessed, Holy book
For every honest seeker, life within

GODHEAD, THREE IN ONE
May 9, 2014

God the Father glorious, pristine, ageless, sublime.
Jesus Christ, Begotten Son, descended into time.
Holy Spirit reticent, sweet messenger divine.
Holy Godhead, three in one, our Savior,
    yours and mine.

Our Father had a purpose, and of course He has it still,
vast sons like His begotten one,
    surrendered to His will.
To fill His royal kingdom, they would all be His delight,
where sun and moon no longer shine,
    God's Glory giveth light.

Lord Jesus Christ, victorious, defeated Satan's curse,
with His many membered body He will
    fill the universe.
The day and hour are hidden but are
    settled well ahead,
when Christ will fulfill prophecy, resuscitate the dead.

God's Holy Spirit will receive a habitation sure,
right here on earth, a many membered temple,
    sweet and pure.
Each living stone comprising an eternal temple, where
God's Holy Spirit liveth, though He liveth everywhere.

So here we see the Godhead, although three,
    yet ever one,
pre-existing ere existence in the past was e'en begun.
The Alpha and Omega, the beginning and the end,
with the plan for all creation, as Jehovah did intend.

And thus, the triune Godhead as presented
    in God's Word,
will bring about the Will of God,
    to those who haven't heard.
Presented, that accepting Christ
    each sinner might obtain
salvation, with deliverance from Hell's eternal flame.

DYING IS EASY, LIVING IS HARD
May 4, 2014

Dyin' is easy, livin' is hard, to quote the remarks
of some unrevealed bard.
But I know what he meant, 'cause I too felt that way
after my God event, on that wonderful day.

Now what, you may ask, is he talkin' about,
did he sample that flask he seems never without.
Yes, I did drink a lot, that used to be true,
but I don't anymore, I'll explain it to you.

I was sitting alone on that wonderful morn,
Christ reached down from heaven and I was reborn.
Oh, I could not re-enter my own Mother's womb,
my Spirit was reborn, to be ever in tune.

My marriage was broken, my wife still in bed,
to that dust covered Bible, my spirit was led.
I just opened it up and read one little verse,
when the heavens exploded, to break Satan's curse.

As I sat bewildered, God poured out from above,
an encompassing flood of His heavenly love.
Oh, I knew it was God, Be assured when I say,
Once you're touched by God, there is no other way.

So, by "dyin' is easy", you can see what I mean,
when I die I'll have fountains of God's love, serene.
And by "livin' is hard", I mean it's hard to wait,
'till the day I can enter God's heavenly estate.

A NEW MIND
May 8, 2014

When is the die then cast in a new mind?
A child is born, influence will now begin,
the unintentional forces, pressed in kind
that determine over many years
if this new mind will one day lose or win.

Lose or win, not in life's obvious games
but rather, in unrecognised challenges of life
that manifest in strength, when lust inflames
or not, to lose or else to win, financially
when winning often brings destructive strife.

That childish mind which tempts us to indulge,
to then allow the seeds of selfishness to feed
on our permissiveness. Oh, not to every need
but rather, every hidden greediness,
that tends to flaunt in every grasping want.

But he's so cute I hear you say, however to resist
such sweet, imploring innocence,
that tiny grasping fist.
I just can't stand to see him cry, when just as easily
it's in my power to mollify, to grant each wish.

Fast forward now, plus fifteen years or so,
our baby's grown and now he's never home.
The friends he keeps do give us pause,
    where does he go;
we hesitate to interfere because, we surely know
a raging fight ensues,
    whene'er he cannot get his own.

The kindness that permissiveness displays,
    is poisonous,
not kindness, but destruction in those seeds we sow.
If we mould a mind God places in the care of us,
to learn when discipline rewards a tantrum fuss
and rear him in the fear of God, then watch him gro

OVERWHELMING LOVE
May 3, 2014

We just don't get it,
there comes from above
Indescribably, overwhelmingly
beautiful love.

Love that man can't describe,
the words don't exist,
and could never compare
with a sweetheart's first kiss.

And this love that our Lord
doth pour into our heart,
has no limits with man,
we can all have a part.

But you have to relax
for your heart to attest,
focus in on our Savior,
God will do the rest.

Just speak the name Jesus,
for right from the start,
Christ Jesus stands waiting
to give you His heart.

How can the God
who spoke all into being,
visit six billion hearts
without some disagreeing.

Your tenure on earth
cannot be a rehearsal.
We are all to be judged,
it's a fact, universal.

So, choose Jesus now,
While you still have a choice.
Christ Jesus will hear you,
He longs for your voice.

IT'S KILL OR BE KILLED
April 27, 2014

War, war, let's even the score,
let's kill those bastards, we'll hurt them sore.
The tension thickens, propaganda excites,
babies just born won't see many more nights.

We're just going about our own business and then,
another war seems to be starting again.
The economy lags, needs a shot in the arm,
might kill a few million, so where's all the harm.

Every red blooded eighteen year old's hot to begin,
how stirring his uniform, handsome and slim.
His rifle and bayonet shiny and bright,
he's well trained how to shoot
    and he's spoiling to fight.

Load up the troop-ships, send them all over there.
Over there, over there, send the word over there
that the dead are coming, the dead are coming
and they won't come back when it's over, over there.

They'll die in their youth and they'll die in their fright,
they were brave, oh so brave
    in their strength and their might.

Upon that command they came over the top,
and they vowed they'd advance
    till they won or they dropped.

And then through the mist what is this that I see,
it's the enemy charging, they look just like me.
They're only scared kids, but they have to advance,
both sides are so scared that we're messing our pants.

But it's kill or be killed as I rip out his guts,
he falls with a scream to the earth that abuts
the mad world that exists betwixt that boy and me,
his wide staring eyes scream an unspoken plea.

Then when we come to the end of the war,
matters not who killed who, we were happy before.
Now we suffer on both sides from battle fatigue,
while the winners are those who devised this intrigue.

TRAGEDY OF LIFE
May 9, 2014

Lazily, the serried seagulls bank and turn
in sweeping circles through the rain washed air.
How brightly on my vision, sun doth brightly burn
at tide's low ebb, revealing sandy reaches bare.

The morning freshened as the clouds withdrew
in scudding strands of wispy, tattered cirrus.
All nature danced to celebrate another day,
    brand new,
becoming all, both large and small, delirious.

The tragedy of life and death in rank devise
displaying cold indifference, as a seagull slew
a fledgling, innocently taken by complete surprise,
before the merest taste of life, he knew.

And just as creatures lives intrude and leave
this busy stage called life without regret.
How many thousands every day must grieve
the deaths of men, whom God didst once beget.

Man was not made for death, nor made for strife,
what tragedy befalls mans sinful way.
Whom God designed to never die, eternal life,
and will restore, when Christ returns one day.

MINDS UNLEASHED
May 2, 2014

Full many a poet's born to bloom unseen,
to waste his visions, on the desert air.
Full many a poet puts to verse, his dream,
to flaunt before blind masses,
masses ever unaware.

Closeted in darkness, clothed in mystery,
a mind if shackled by disuse or fear
might atrophy and wither to a stricken thing,
devoid of all Intent and yet,
it might have hatched a king.

Of all the things we lose, the mind
must be life's greatest loss of all.
It's not that we refuse, but find
we suffocate beneath life's deadly pall.

The mind unleashed might rise on silver wings,
to bring to life, things hitherto unknown.
The mind released denies no higher things,
than are imagined in one mind alone.

And so, when thoughts unbidden come to mind,
do not reject them, they might be the start
of some enormous revelation, blind as yet to truth,
but striving to at last escape the heart.

SUPERFICIAL DEATH
April 30, 2014

Have you noticed, how unintendedly
superficially we see death.
We would not of course, intend to see
death so decidedly casually,
if it's us, as we draw our last breath.

But if it were us, there would be no fuss,
for of course, we're unable to know
when we must die, so no time to cry,
else we'd sure see those teardrops flow.

It's not that we're mean, it's just that we seem
unable to anguish for others.
I mean folks we don't know, not our family below,
our dear siblings or fathers or mothers.

Perhaps on T.V. we might happen to see,
a bomb blast showing terrible views.
Our head sees the dead but our heart is not led
to deep grief, we just watch other news.

Yet the truth, sad to state, when we just can't relate,
there are others whose grief is extreme.
Being closely related, as formerly stated,
they are living a terrible dream.

But the end of it all, just to hear our Lord call,
come up hither, see what is to come.
If we embrace our Lord, we'll be all one accord,
in God's presence forever, each one.

GOD OF THE LIVING
April 26, 2014

When we vacate this earth so fair
And travel to our just reward
Will weepers seek us, will they care
Or discard us with one accord

What have I with thee, Jesus said
To remonstrate with rebuke severe
I rule the living, not the dead
Dost thou the living God revere

The living are the ones in Christ
The rest who walk about are dead
Who acquiesced when sin enticed
Who followed meek when Satan led

We who are Christ's will blithely bind
Our destiny to Jesus care
Releasing all we left behind
Of earthly gold, earthly despair

Sojourn on earth doth garner men
Beloved families and friends
But we must hold them loosely when
All earthly interchange suspends

WHEN THAT LIGHT TURNETH ON
April 22, 2014

When our heart holds a place without Christian faith
Are we free
Oh, we're free in the sense we pay no recompense
To the truths we can't see
But truth has a way at the end of one's day
Of sweeping cobwebs of confusion away
Revealing to one where the basis of faith might be

The freedom then gained bringeth light
    to a darkened place
With bewilderment flowing,
    there's no way of knowing
All truth that was hid is now free
But the point now unspoken, how evil was broken
To bring new believers to be
Is a gift from above bestowed with God's love
Enabling a doubter to see

When that light turneth on, all confusion is gone
God removeth the scale from blind eyes
Joy is birthed in man's heart, he is now at the start
Of sunshiny days when God's mercy betrays
The deception that Satan bestows with a will
On all seekers of truth with a vengeance until
Christ arrival bodes evil's depart

GOD'S NAME NOT IN VAIN
April 19, 2014

"FOR GOD'S SAKE", you hear it expressed
When they're really surprised, that says it best
With profanity though, God is not concerned
The end result that's eventually earned
Is when souls are blessed

Or "GO TO HELL" is commonly told
Unthinkingly from a heart that's cold
The consequence if that curse were applied
And the supplicant was the one who died
Is too horrible to behold

Or "FOR CHRIST'S SAKE" is a curse they tell
When it's not for His sake, as we know well
Addressing a cause with the name of our Lord
That penetrates with the power of His word
Might save a soul from hell

Or "GOD DAMN YOU" would never fly
From a heart, not knowing the reason why
God does not damn, but will always bless
May GOD BLESS YOU, is the way to success
Why not give it a try

Basis of each curse by its very name
Suggests from the root of worship it came
Man doth God's name unknowing conspire
To bring before God's angelic choir
Stirring angels to worship God again

All things, God worketh together for good
Cursing or blessing, God understood
God knoweth, they know not what they say
Men are blind to truth, Satan leadeth astray
But God saves men who awake and repent,
If they only would

TRADE GOLD FOR DROSS
April 16, 2014

This world where we reside is hard and cold
The Spirit world contrasts, so soft and warm
That world wherein God doth reside
Though hidden, God doth sometime guide
A stranger seeking shelter from life's storm

But when we seek, we mostly cannot find
Why Thou withholdeth, we believe we know
We willfully demandeth more
While forgetting that which went before
Those moments once arrayed in golden glow

That which is holy, we are so inclined
To trample underfoot in afterthought
That which Thou didst deign to show
With time doth fade in afterglow
While seeking more, the former comes to naught

And so the gold we find, we trade for dross
Believing we deserve a greater gift
We are the center after all
Though others might embrace the fall
We do epitomize wisdom and thrift

Because God understands and doth forgive
Our sins He loves to cleanse, to touch our hearts
Will lead us blindly to the truth
Despite man's foolishness, forsooth
Right here on earth, ere consciousness departs

WHERE ARE YOU, LORD JESUS
March 29, 2014

Where are You, Lord Jesus, are You
    out beyond the stars,
would we find You there, Lord Jesus,
    out past Jupiter, past Mars?
If we could we would, invade men's hearts,
    determine their intent,
and if we did not find You there,
    would we know where You went?

If we passed the sickly beggar,
    sprawling at the rich man's gate,
would You be there to stroke his hair,
    or would we still have to wait?
Or if we're led to a hospital bed,
    where a sinner fights for breath,
if she gasps your name, will she die in shame,
    or be sanctified at death?

Where, oh where, for those hearts that care,
    are you hiding, precious Lord,
are You still the same as the day you came,
    to reveal Yourself, God's Word?
Do you still relate at each rich man's gate,
    to each Lazarus lying, sore,
does Your love extend to the very end
    for each sinner, lost in war?

There's no guarantee for you and me,
    that Jesus is really true,
except in each heart where Christ has a part,
    in me, as I hope in you.
I've heard every excuse to evade the truth,
    and each one at the end is lost,
so we beg of you, since Christ be true,
    don't reject Him, a terrible cost.

Will we stand at the end, on ourselves depend,
    and stoutly defy God,
will we stand with pride, and refuse to abide,
    on truths the angels applaud?
Our defiance in life, a bombastic device,
    to justify man as boss,
but we'll understand well at the entrance to Hell,
    Salvation's terrible loss.

WHAT BOLDNESS BIRTHS
April 15, 2014

What boldness births within the heart of one
Who, having only ever just begun
To question all creation's manifest
Begins to focus in on evidence he only guessed
Could never be undone

The query who am I, adds further to the question
Also aids his indigestion, simply why
Why am I, what reason might he find to thus inform
To shed some light to brighten up the endless night
That ever tries, prevents, denies, the morn

The groaning in his gut, doth imitate creation's groan
His spirit man doth suffer with all creation's pain
He is manifesting sympathetic birth pangs
    yet unknown
As creation brings to birth, God's resurrected earth
Pristine again

When God's Holy Spirit opens up his blinded eyes
God's Holy Word will fill that empty void
If he now keeps quiet, the stones must then cry out
For sin repealed as God revealed,
    he has to sing and shout
Hell's curse on him forever now destroyed

SECTION TWO
Humorous Poetry

SECRETS OF GOD
Aug. 2, 2015

There are secrets that God doth bandy about,
but in secret of course, so we don't find out.
Not that God doth fear shedding info. abroad,
it's because He don't want us to think we're God,
don't you think.

Like, what secret power informs, think ye
when thousands of birds all flying be.
In total unison, banking in flight,
how can each know, to the left or the right,
think ye.

Or when, deep in the ground a flower grows,
How can it know it will be a rose.
As a little dry seed when it started life,
how could it contain that smell so nice,
would you suppose.

By the thousands, frail butterfly's travel south,
are they told when to go, by word of mouth.
Then they die down south while their babies roam,
who imparts the locale of their northern home,
think ye.

Scientists be in charge of the answers, I fear,
but they can't fly with swallows and insects, I hear.
In examples of life we ask, right from its start,
can science reveal how God gave them life's spark,
do you think.

EACH LOVELY FLAME
Aug. 2, 2015

When God placed in man
a desire for sex,
and then fashioned
a lovely woman next.
Did He understand
that He placed in man,
a desire to expect
to catch if he can,
each lovely temptress
his lusting saw.

If he had to he might
even break the law,
and be willing to fight
for each lovely flame,
then temporarily
forget his shame,
tho every desire
as it came to bud
was turning his name
the color of mud.

God of course knew,
at the very begin,
that's why He inserted
a conscience in,
so that man would focus
his mind on God
to control himself,
then God would win.

WHEN FALLING IN LOVE
Aug. 1, 2015

When two people fall into each other,
they of course, fall in love with the flesh.
But there has to be more to discover,
when two lives contemplate an enmesh.

No doubt, they will not even know it,
since the falling in love is so sweet.
But if they're ever going to grow it,
after they're swept off their feet,

there must come a much deeper sensation,
where they give it some second thought.
It might come as a revelation,
contemplating the book that each bought.

Each book had such a beautiful cover,
they engaged it with nary a care.
But to ever grow love for each other,
they each have to be very aware,

of the other's inner requirements,
read discerningly, between the lines.
They be deeper, unsaid, not casually read,
nor just featured in bed, betimes.

At the last, there must be sure foundation,
for two love's to be builded upon.
Jesus must abide there, for each lover to share
blessings here and in heaven anon.

CUPPA TEA
July 29, 2015

Sun sets,
darkness falls again
as I sit by my lonely
window pane,
and hark to the echo
footsteps make,
hurrying home
because its late.

Thoughts percolate
within my head,
are they simply
hurrying home
to bed,
or is someone
waiting at home
to greet,
with a cosy fire
to warm their feet.

I turn again
to my empty room,
and long for
the sound
of a busy broom
or the loving gift
of a cup of tea.
But I'm hit with
This cold reality;
No love will ever
again agree,
to share this room
with God and me.

GOD'S EVERYWHERE LOVE
July 28, 2015

I see God's love in a buzzing bee,
bequeathing honey's benevolence.
And equally, spreading His largesse,
I see it in chicken's eggs, no less.

But I see it too, in the beauty laid
on a pristine lawn that is freshly cut.
God's beauty reflected in every blade,
if I raise my eyes above life's rut.

So beauty, in eye of beholder doth lie,
depending they tell me, on how we look.
In the blue portrayed by a cloudless sky,
God's love's displays like an open book.

Some others hate bees because they sting,
but isn't that a reflection of life.
Sometimes the sweetness of life doth bring
from bee's other end, a little strife.

And the grass from sun, might eventually lie
raggedy brown from potential drought.
Half empty some cups become, bye and bye,
then the half that remains, begins pouring out.

So, I hate to tell you, but feel I must,
You're the only one to determine your fate.
Look up, don't look down, in Jesus trust,
you must do it now, before it's too late.

GODLY TREES
July 28, 2015

Did ya ever, with Godly trees converse
whenever, forests you blithely traverse,
who knew.
If you tell on me, they'll think I'm daft,
that I'm losing aholt of me native craft,
like some o' you.

Comin' back to the trees, they do talk you know,
not so much in winter when muffling snow
doth silence trees.
But in summer when covered in fluttering leaves,
you'd almost think the folk strollin' below,
they're tryin' to please.

And they live a lot longer than some o' you,
which is not too hard of a thing to do,
if ya knows what I means.
So, thru all those years, they have learned to talk,
but they needs you to listen, when out for a walk
by foresty streams.

I knows talkin' to trees can be met with a scoff,
with folk thinkin' you're tryin' to put them off,
I'm in good company tho, whilst talkin to trees.
I have no doubt, when out for a walk,
that God and trees might engage in talk,
God could use the breeze.

MAN'S DEBACLE
July 27, 2015

This arena man inhabits, didst array
God's creation, beautifully content.
Man's arrival, could not long delay
sin's subtle, vile intrusion,
into goodness, to futilely circumvent.

Doth God despair! Of course not!
God reigns in sweet perfection there
in heaven's pristine beauty where
God sustains high over us, impervious.
Yet, a miracle past understanding,
God Doth Care.

Did our malfeasance take God by surprise?
If I said yes, wouldst ignorance display.
God's plan reached further down the years
than paradise at first appears,
e'en Rome, God did not build in just a day.

Some folk proclaim, there never was a God,
then famously, this contradiction bring.
An Act Of God's how man describes
destruction, when their sin collides
with Godly law, distorting everything.

Each man's debacle, thru the years
which sin didst constitute, God saw
I have no doubt, at its begin.
For Jesus Christ, God didst suspend
to slash the Cross, through every loss
succeeding mankind's sin.

AH, SWEET BUTTERFLY
July 31, 2015

Ah, sweet butterfly,
wouldst that thou wert mine,
but God didst otherwise ordain.
Thy beauty, illuminating sky's
monotony, couldst not contain
man's clumsiness, but must be free.
Such beauty must not limit
to man's greed but must constrain,
never man to touch but only see.
Butterflies appear for us
from secret, hidden bower
where delicately, butterflies are made.
Enthralling us for just the hour
thru summer sun, to then
obtain again, that hidden glade
from whence they erstwhile come.
Ah butterfly, to hold thee my desire,
but were I to touch, thy radiant beauty
wouldst expire, and so,
I must consume thy beauty from afar.
Farewell, my lovely flying star.

SPLIT PERSONALITIES
July 25, 2015

Our brains be divided in two,
hemisphere right and hemisphere left.
Tho each hemisphere is all about you,
personality wise, you be cleft.

The left side deals with the here and now,
the immediacy of all around you.
The right side can be likened to la-la-land,
where you'll be when God has found you.

The left side is busy with coming and going,
whether running or standing still.
The right side is inclined to gather our mind
into visions, wherever it will.

The right side can deliver you into a view
of loveliness, absent from stress.
Where you'll venture free of the world to see
how God's waiting, our lives to bless.

Tho the left side too, is needed to do
all the tasks that require our time.
But strive to escape, thru the right side's gate
to envision contentment, Divine.

WHAT HIDES INSIDE
July 25, 2015

Boy meets girl, that old, old song,
he sees her, thinks he knows her well.
Girl thinks, with him she could belong,
within her heart, rings wedding bell,
but what doth hide unseen.

Girl falls in love with what she sees,
with boy, her lovely form drew him.
She brings him closer by degrees,
he knows her well, doth venture in,
but what doth hide unseen.

Their flesh doth certainly entice,
he's strong and handsome to the core.
What each can see is very nice,
but as proposed to you before,
what doth hide unseen.

To truth reveal, I'll now begin
the best, kept to the last for you.
MAN'S SPIRIT percolates within,
God sent it, down to earth it flew,
to hide inside, unseen.

So spirit, is what each didst woo,
though each might never know.
Spirit, partly wouldst leak through,
but visibly, didst rarely show
what strove inside, unseen.

WRINKLED OLD YOU
July 24, 2015

A man named Abram, a Godly man,
and his childless wife, Sarai,
dwelt in a land called Canaan Land,
by God, and not by Abram planned,
so that's where they tented to stay.

Abram was accosted by God one day,
as he lolled around in the sand.
Thy name be now called Abraham,
thy wife Sarah be no longer Sarai, and
she'll soon be in the family way.

Now Abraham, nigh unto ninety nine,
was long past the desire for a kid.
Deep in his heart, he gasped a guffaw
for his wife was ninety years old, he saw,
and of nurseries, he was well rid.

Didst God e'er tell you, the same words true,
I'm sure you'd respond in kind.
If God told you're wife, she'd pregnant be
next year when she's maybe, ninety three,
you might both go outa' your mind.

In my mental picture, there's wrinkled old you
on your hands and knees, going cootchy coo
to a wrinkled old baby boy.
Let's wipe that right out, God is not about
To repeat, that was one of a kind.

I PRETEND I'M A SAGE
July 22, 2015

Life holds a strange attraction,
to all the years tip toeing before.
Now that life looks to transpire,
all the lust and the fire,
disappears like a burned out war.

Reflection takes root like a habit,
a habit acquired looking back.
We're now able to see
the transparencies we
would employ to salve conscience' attack.

Word transparencies use, is really a ruse
I employ, because sin sounds so bad.
When younger, I wasn't aware of sin,
not as much as I now seem reflective in,
since no longer, much sin's to be had.

I now pretend I'm a sage since, about middle age
Christ Jesus didst apprehend me.
Too soon I got old; too late I got wise,
too soon I portrayed my insufferable disguise,
but at last God has made me free.

So if you're old like me, or even if you are not,
screw up your courage, reach out to God.
Your whole world will change,
God will in time rearrange
your priorities, as angels applaud.

MY ACTIVITY IS MOSTLY CEREBRAL
July 8, 2014

When we reach my age which is 88,
    most activity is cerebral,
Oh, I walk a bit but not too much,
    and other than that, I just meditate.
As I sat in my garden one summer day,
    as I often do I hasten to say
it occurred to me that as persons we,
    see ourselves most importantly,
and why not, if I care not for little ol' me,
    who else is gonna relate,
that might sound selfish but really it's not,
    it's built into our d.n.a.

But I made a mighty effort at last,
    to force my attention away
from myself, and tried to imagine how God
    might think of men today.
He's seen other men in other climes,
    in other ages, other times,
multiplied billions o'er centuries,
    who appeared but now are gone,
each one would have this d.n.a. built in,
    self preservation must go on.

As I sat in my garden reverie,
    God's first Bible book came to mind,
Genesis is the name man appended to it,
    led by the Holy Ghost.
I went inside to Bible retrieve,
    my memory's shortened would you believe,
and in chapter one, verse 27,
    were the words that I savored the most.
So God created man in His image,
    in the image of God created He him,
male and female created He them,
    so women feverishly began to conceive.

The result is the mess that we're in today,
    tho our pedigree ranks so high,
but that is the reason that Jesus came,
    in case you were wondering why,
God knew we were lost and to pay the cost,
    our Savior consented to die.
God gave His Only Begotten Son,
    who was prophesied from of old,
we subsequently became adopted sons,
    in the Bible we are told.

Now the point I would make since it's getting late,
    why does God care such a lot.
we're made in God's image but how do we act,
    just like the Devil and that's a fact,
I pray God will never decide to retract,
    I don't wanna go down where its hot.
I'm just kidding around, in the Bible 'tis found,
    God stays the same, never changes,
Bible truth that's revealed is eternally sealed,
    just exactly how God arranges.

MEMORY LOSS
September 2, 2014

I'm off to shop for her once more
to purchase choice viands.
Selecting only her specific, sore
demands.

The cold wore thin as, seeking more
of memory whilst traveling,
With mem'ry fast unravelling,
I swore!

Oh, nothing grave or blasphemous
wouldst e'er dispel my fear of God.
I couldst not laud, nor e'er applaud
sin fast enough!

But as I journeyed thru the cold,
I wracked my brain for inspiration.
Forgetting items, I was told
kills adulation!

Then just as I achieved the store
and saw what they were selling.
Memory clicked, I never swore,
when I get home, there'll be no more
loud yelling!

FAITHLESS AND PERVERSE
September 13, 2014

"Oh faithless and perverse generation
How long shall I be with you and suffer you"...
In this, Jesus was clearly annoyed with us
By "us", I include every subsequent man
Not just the disciples who then followed Him
But all since who've agreed with His plan

"Lord I believe, help thou mine unbelief"
Describes the whole gang of us clear
We say we believe and we mean what we say
Or we think we do but then one day
While we strain to be very sincere
Along comes temptation when guard is down
"pride of life" bites us right in the rear

Our Lord Jesus Christ sits in His heavenly place
At the Father's right hand, enthroned
Doth He look down on man who He never disowned
For the bible says God never changes
And still call us perverse when He hears us curse
As our destiny, He arranges

Thank God He forgives and permits us to live
Until finally, we come to our senses
If He took us too soon there would be a great boon
Of lost souls when His judgement commences
So we'd best soon awake to the truth we forsake
If we're still without Christ, no defences

GOD HAS A PLACE FOR YOU
August 15, 2014

Upon a day so far away
The God-man came to earth
Clothed in flesh that man might say
'Twas just a normal birth

The God I laud will e'er display
Grand majesty to flaunt
That demonstrates the deity
Of Gods, as is their wont

You can't fool me, I am you see
Endowed with intellect
No baby from a mother's womb
As god, wouldst man suspect

What god would slip in unawares
To claim his regal place
Would he not be proceeded by
Processions full of grace

Must he not be the focus of
Great worship and respect
To ultimately gather in
Those fortunes he'd collect

I will not bend, I will not bow
I will not act the fool
To worship fleshly man as god
A babe to puke and drool

But hark! I hear an angel choir
Extolling Him as God
I'm wrong! So wrong, my heart's on fire
Their worship I applaud

I cannot wait, it's not too late
To worship Jesus too
We all must shun a sinner's fate
God has a place for you

CONSCIOUSNESS
July 21, 2014

So what is consciousness anyway,
and how much of it do we retain.
How much and of what, have we consciousness,
what unconsciousness yet doth remain.

And what about so called lower levels of life,
of what doth their consciousness vie.
Is awareness of spider's culinary delight
in the consciousness held by a fly.

Caterpillars transform into butterflies, yet
are they conscious that they have to try.
Did they know it was coming and simply forget,
then unconsciously learn how to fly.

Did they stand on a branch and then simply by chance
when a breeze came along, wave their arms.
Would they simply not know,
    those are wings down below,
as they fly over cities and farms.

And when people are born, it is surely the norm
that we're empty of consciousness.
We're just full of the things
    that unconsciousness brings,
Our whole life is unconsciousness.

But how quickly we learn, to unconsciousness spurn,
we're then conscious of food when we cry.
We learn big people snore, two plus two equals four,
we can consciously walk if we'll try.

Consciousness we retain 'cause God gave us a brain,
evident in most people, I guess.
Then our consciousness spreads into
    other folks heads,
'till we're conscious of each other's mess.

AFFAIRS OF LIFE
June 24, 2014

The affairs of life that occupy,
most of the focus of you and I
as the years go on, and gently pass
away.

Have much to do with the comfort of
our body, the center of our love.
Will our fancy dinner be under glass
today.

Have we lost an inch or gained a pound,
we must be careful to not surround
ourselves with the stuff to surfeit
each selfish need.

The focus and purpose of every thought
is inward turned, as its central plot
proposes to glut and we will not, turf it
for greed.

Why do we struggle, why do we care,
as selfishness manifests everywhere.
If the space we fill found its empty self
without

Our negligent presence, would any note
if we're not in the now, to grandly emote
or to make a fuss, to scrabble for wealth
or shout.

This poem depicts my most selfish view,
but Christ will forgive each one of you
who repents, He will gladly bestow a new
Selfless Eternal Life.

THIS THING DISEASE
June 21, 2014

Lord, the thought occurred just the other day,
it's kind of foolish, but what can I say.
It's the creative guise, the inventiveness,
that You grant to get us out of this mess
with relative ease...
This thing DISEASE.

Lord, we do have an endless variety,
with a great deal more to spare.
Some of it's even happened to me,
which seems unfair, for You know I care.
It really does hurt and it makes me swear,
if you please.

Really, most of it hurts and some makes us halt,
though we know of course, that it's not Your fault.
We know as well you could make a change,
our susceptible wont to each dastardly curse,
You could rearrange, so it don't get worse,
how strange.

For it seems to me, though I'm just a man,
You could change all this, Oh I know You can.
Instead of the trouble You must go through
to inspire research for each cure, then You
could take away all of man's disease
with a spoken word, it would really please
this scurvy crew.

And You wouldn't then have to work so hard,
teaching us how to cure our ills.
You could then endear us with true regard,
with a word you could clean our messes and spills.
You could watch as our sickness in life distills,
and make everything work for this hapless bard,
this inept retard.

HORMONAL DIALOGUE
June 14, 2014

Have you ever wondered what's in mans eye
That makes sex so darned attractive
Why it seems to always, ever try
To make men's libido active

We harbor no secret desire to sin
At least most of us don't, I believe
So why inside, when a woman walks in
Do our hormones strive to achieve

She doesn't resemble a movie star
But imagination's at work
While our deep insides, where conscience resides
Make us start to feel like a jerk

We mentally render ourselves, a kick
In the place where its gonna hurt
This deflates our libido effectively quick
Removing temptation to flirt

I'm sure you will find, television's designed
To keep that desire aglow
Those attractive girls with their bouncing curls
Are intended to tempt, I know

But its harmless enough, we tell ourselves
As we savor lascivious thought
Jesus does not agree, for the bible told me
That adultery's the charge when caught

We will not be able to lie in the day
That we stand in the presence of God
For God will wipe all pretenses away
As His angels stand and applaud

ONE DAY IN SCRIPTURE
April 21, 2014

One day in ancient scripture stated,
Israelites with breath abated, fled from
alien shores well hated, to the shores
of infamy. As they hastened to be free of,
captors without least degree of, pity or
much hope to see love, emanate in sympathy.
Egyptian's well developed system, testified
by much encryption, to their highly vaunted
wisdom, rated to the nth degree. Then when
everything seemed lost in, Israelites forlornly
tossed in, all the facts that they could muster,
sad of face with little luster, sad to see.
Egyptian hordes began to close in, God divinely
spoke to those in, charge and who would hear.
namely Moses at the head of, Godly hordes who
bravely fed love, to each other strong instead of,
weakening fear. Then to everyone's surprise,
events that no one could surmise, credulity
filled people's eyes, at what their leader did.
Moses staff raised threateningly, as never once
before did he, and suddenly the hordes could see,
God, the waters bid. The waters did divide in two,
allowing them to travel through, and then before
Egyptians knew, their quarry got away. Boldly they
did follow dry shod, through the sea divided by God,
but they never could comply broad, enough

BOB MCCLUSKEY

that fateful day. Israelites reached the other shore,
and saw Egyptians fated sore, could not escape
the sea before, it swept them all away. Israelites
now with faith restored, God nevermore would
be ignored, each day on bended knee implored,
God to forever stay. History though doth yet reveal,
commands of God lost all appeal, Israelites forgot
to kneel, and wouldn't stop to pray. The day is coming
soon we know, God's Spirit over them will flow,
rebellion then will truly go, away.

RANDOM FOOLISHNESS
April 9, 2014

I came, I saw, I squandered
And then put it all to rhymes
Imagination wandered
Uninhibited, betimes

When life began, I now realize
End was already in sight
The interim suffered with shuttered eyes
But nearer the end, delight

To experience uncontrollable rage
Just threaten a mother's babe
You'll never live to be old enough
To march in the veteran's parade

When a poet's brand new
He might borrow from you
While a poet mature
From theft will not demure
While denying it's true

Modern art has the capacity
To threaten ones brain with explosion
Each brain's much the same
But the name of the game's
Intercept intellectual corrosion

Information is quite necessary
To accumulate, we know
But it curdles my blood
In the midst of this flood
Where did all of God's wisdom go

We are God's musical instruments
Through which God, each symphony plays
God of course would assume
Though we're oft out of tune
We'll express our Lord's best, Polonaise

FOOLISH THOUGHTS
April 5, 2014

God's perfection affords protection
From creative carelessness
A forgetful wave of His hand could bring
A greater travail to man's suffering
I guess

I can't help but think, a forgetful blink
Of God's eye could mean
Another bump on the road of life
To add to the sum of a sinners strife
Through life's careen

Or a hastily uttered creative command
And we all would fall, no one could stand
As we flop around on rubbery legs
Like kneeling kids playing mumblety pegs
In a fairy land

Imagination's a wonderful thing
We can dream of forever becoming kings
Or anything else we might desire
But from foolishness we soon would tire
For grief it brings

Thank God we can trust and I know we must
Refrain from becoming a fool
All those foolish imaginings show there are those
Who would follow the paths of sin, I suppose
Thank God for His manifest rule

SPIRITUAL REALITY
March 31, 2014

Which reality is real
And not just a sub-set
Created for God's purpose true
There's a spiritual reality
That will one day let,
Life extend betwixt heaven and you

Oh, I know just how real
Our existence doth feel
That hammer is harder than stone
But there's more open space
In that hammer, that place
Than the atoms that fill it alone

Now I can't testify that I've studied
To try, scientifically to prove absolute
That a heaven exists, but when my wife kissed
The first time, no discourse could refute
For the distance you see, creates no divide
That reality true, walks right alongside

So, a Christian, the day he must go heavens way
Might not have to travel far
Heaven's Spiritual place just inhabits his space
God simply appears from afar
We do not have to wait, can't be early or late
For time flees, when God fills where we are

EACH MOMENT LOST
March 31, 2014

The moments flow
The "now" we know, departs
Noiselessly, quite unobserved
By six billion beating hearts
Each moment bequeathed
Will not repeat
It just silently imparts
Its contribution
To the time we served

In the larger scheme of things
One moment matters not
Except of course
If the present one
Is the last one of the lot
When all the moments total up
with all their joys and tears
they clandestinely coalesce
into this pile of years

Were we to know
As moments go
Which moment was the last
Would moments then
Be savored well
As clocks and watches

Tick to tell
Would we restrain
The clocks refrain
From flowing quite so fast

But as I add a little thought
What matters, times depart
I plan to go to a place I know
In the center of Jesus heart
When I die I win
Christ will let me in
So let the moments flow
Choose Jesus too
I beg of you
Don't end up, down below

MAN OVER WOMAN
July 30, 2015

Overwhelming saturation comes to man,
the consequence of woman's loveliness.
Which, outside of marriage, God doth ban,
oft consumed whene'er presented, non-the-less.

The bible states that over woman, man be head,
in most of life's endearments, this be true.
But in the situation hinted at, let it be said,
Most women hold great power over you.

Man is most assuredly much stronger than his mate,
and this is as it should be, I suspect.
But when the wife coquettishly endeavors to relate,
All manly fortitude's completely wrecked.

That might be as it should be,
    to populate the human race,
for to fill the earth, man needs must multiply.
But sin can be a consequence God seeketh to erase,
Which brings us to the present you and I.

Sin ravages in every land, may God forgive us all,
as savages and civilized, God seeks to reprimand.
The Moslems overcome this,
    being draped from head to toe,
then no one can suspect a sin,
    still raging out of hand.

I know God has made a way for me,
    I read it in the Bible,
repent and ask Lord Jesus to come in.
It's there for everyone to see and everyone is liable,
the Blood of Christ will cleanse each sinner
    from his sin.

SATAN'S WINDY HOUR
July 29, 2015

Behold,
the simple vestiges of change,
precipitating cold, or even wet,
when heaven's dark, doth rearrange
the windy rivers flowing overhead.

And yet,
those windy rivers sometime follow evil plan,
to move not from change of temperature,
which must not ordinarily, bow to any
feeble effort from the hand of man.

Behold,
a Man once stood in bold defiance of the rude
effects which unruly temperature didst intrude,
in bold reliance on a power in abeyance kept
by righteousness, to be revealed in time.

And yet,
God's curtain parted slightly in that fateful hour,
lending credence to God's revelation
of a dispensation new, revealing power
over sin, if man wouldst but submit to God.

Behold,
man witnessed on that day, recorded well,
Satan's interrupting, windy power.
God's Holy Spirit, didst that power deflate
as Jesus Christ stood tall against debate,
commanding Satan's windy hour,
PEACE, BE STILL!

JUDGEMENT INTENSE
September 12, 2014

I will go one day
And it may be soon
On a heavenly journey
Far past the moon

Or might it be just a sideways step
Through the curtain of life
That evades us yet
But will be here soon

For that other world
Where God resides
Might be just over the hill
In a manner of speaking
Still

What will I be like then
Or for that matter, you
Will we be old and feeble
When you'll still be you

Maybe younger and handsomer
With nary an infirmity
Will you look again like you used to look
At twenty three

One thing I know
When we have to go
We'll be stripped of all pretense
Nowhere to hide
From the guilt inside
Thru judgement intense

LOVE'S SWEET EMBRACE
August 31, 2014

What blessings didst God impart,
when He gave to every man
a woman's heart to love, apart
from any other kind of love
that Satan might dare to start.

As they come together at last,
what lovely warmth of pure delight,
two blending into one embrace
ecstatically throughout the night,
in love's gentle place.

Then, given passage of time,
their love evolves to a deeper place
where mind of each doth rhyme.
To only observe the other's face
is to know the other's mind.

Man, in his clumsy way doth try
to relate unselfishly.
But selfishness will always out,
the end result, the insensitive lout
will make her cry.

Her bewilderment will pierce like a knife
as he realizes his mistake.
Now full of remorse for the love of his life,
he embraces his weeping, wounded wife
and seeks to reverse his fate.

You only hurt the one you love,
is a line from a well known song.
Forgetting that God in heaven above
forgave them both, for God's pure love
filled each of them all along.

MIND OF MAN
August 13, 2014

The mind can be a strange thing,
    thoughts running to and fro,
a constant rearrange thing,
    wildly dreaming where to go.
No limitations bring constraint, or strive to redirect
a holiday by Air-O-Plane, no air fare to collect.

The mind can be invaded,
    quite divinely it would seem,
whilst waking unexpected,
    or whilst sleeping in a dream.
Enabling us to freely go,
    where man ne'er went before,
enabling whole scenarios of love, of peace, of war.

Creating casts of characters, we ne'er in life have met,
so vividly, as dreams retrieve these lives
    we can't forget.
From whence these interlopers incomplete,
    do they enroll,
are they transcendental hopers,
    searching for a heart or soul?

Do they wander through the ozone,
    deprived of a resting place?

Don't they know there's a no-go-zone,
    in my demented cranial space.
Are they imitating others,
    others whom I've never met.
Do they come from earthly mothers,
    did they have a bassinet?

Do they gather for rehearsal,
    just to practise for each dream,
then after cast dispersal, be rewarded with ice-cream?
And when they aren't working,
    they must stay somewhere, enmasse,
or perhaps they all sit smirking,
    in supernal acting class.

These dreams seem well constructed;
    however doth this come about,
sometimes there is a preacher,
    and he seemeth quite devout.
Wherever did he come from,
    did he go to bible school,
or is he just pretending as he shares the golden rule?

I guess I'd better wrap this up,
    the questions have no end,
these suppositions so obtuse,
    my mind begins to bend.
They say the dreams we dream at night,
    reflect our busy day,
my day's not that exotic, so this can't be true, no way.

DUST CONTAINS NO LIFE
June 19, 2014

We are but dust and yet we love and live
What must dust contain to render love
Most assuredly it is not a composite
Of minerals and elements that lurk
Within the dust, what then doth work
The magic of romance, what chance
Doth bring about the romp of it

Dust contains no life, yet nourisheth
The life containing elemental parts of it
That come from dust, the human bust
Contains, beside the common dust
Intangible, ephemeral , a life that must
Invade the dead and dying dust
Renewing in the start of it
A part of it

And so, we passing dustbins do contain
A heart, a soul, a thinking mind, a brain
What thinketh thou, dost magic intervene
To take the dirt of dust and make it clean
Or dost thou contemplate most solemnly
To bring the dust to life there has to be
A harbinger of life compelling me
To rise up from the state of death to life
The answer's plain, His name is Jesus Christ

IS THERE A CREATOR
August 19, 2014

There are levels of life, almost infinite
right down perhaps, to the atom.
At the insect level for instance,
is a spider conscious of my potential
as a friend instead of as an enemy?
Could we learn to inter-relate
to our mutual enlightenment?
It seems that I possess that potential
but on the face of it, he does not.
Or am I wrong, is he conscious of me
at a higher level than I am aware of;
if I repeatedly brought him food
would he learn not to fear me
and instead learn to even like me.
I wonder if research of this kind
has ever been done and to what extent.
Proceeding to lower levels of consciousness,
from whence, in any "living" organism
does this thing we call life, come?
It appears to be transmitted from one to another
in a never ending chain, but is this really so?
Is the essence, the spark of life independently
presented at some appropriate moment,
from some spiritual or imagined power
or source; and if so, is there therefore a creator?

UNENCUMBERED BY STUFF
August 12, 2014

In a place I like best, I sit ever at rest,
indulging my psyche to roam.
My tilt office chair is quite comforting there,
in this room I regard as my home.

Situate on my right, is the window where light
illuminates with a lovely largesse.
A nice wood lies beyond, but I'm lacking a pond
which would add to my outlook, I guess.

My shelves and odd nooks are encumbered by books,
as computer and printer adorn
my old desk uncomplaining, I feel that I'm gaining
great freedom from stuff long since shorn.

My T.V.'s to my left where I'm gladly bereft
of a player to play D.V.D.s.
This is of no import, for I'm just not the sort
to watch movies for hours, if you please.

At my back is the bed where I rest my wee head,
after midnight when poetry dies.
It's a couch that pulls out, when each night I'm about
to retire, and it's just the right size.

I guess that's about all, there's my art on the wall,
my acrylics do look pretty artsy.
There's a cupboard for clothes,
    where I'm sure you'd propose
I partake, when I haste to departsy.

So other than that, there's a peg for me hat,
plus a dresser for my negligees.
If you seeks me you'll find me,
    with cushions behind me,
in that chair ensconced, most of me days.

MAN'S DOWNWARD TENDENCY
August 11, 2014

All earthly movement floweth downward
as the waters scoureth hills.
Just so, do thoughts of men engage
this downward tendency,
where hidden fleshly lust doth rage
beneath a seeming calm unruffled pool
of subterfuge.

Unseen within, man's finer tendencies submerge
beneath this restless evil flood.
Demanding abject subservience of good
before this unrelenting, heated surge,
where all moral restraint, codified in formal
righteousness lies ignored, indeed defied
by flesh demanding to be fed.

And so, flesh, incessantly hungering for flesh,
will not tolerate denial whilst roiling blood doth boil.
Restraint is sacrificed before the altar of justification
as conscience suffers the searing, desensitizing attack
from unrestrained debauch, to strangle in its coil.
Then finally, as guilt submerges to its hidden place,
mans sin lies hidden well and deep behind his face.

And therein lieth mans overburdened history of sin,
to be it seems, his legacy for evermore.
Not every man to that extent, I hasten to adjure,
but most it seems, because the tempter's garden grows within.
But Jesus gave us victory, with armor to defray
the tempter's fiery arrows as they come our way,
Christ's presence in our hearts doth make us pure.

DEVOURING LOVE
August 5, 2014

God's blooms display prolifically
within man's garden forms.
Alas, the hidden worms
within man's destiny,
devour his latent love for thee,
instilling future storms.

Lost love for thee
devoureth up
thy fairest heart within.
Each future bloom
doth lust consume,
negating yet, with sin.

Within, such love
consumeth hearts
with love which doth devour.
Without revealeth naught
of loss within
each lovely flower.

Consuming sin
of outer man,
doth hope devour.
Whilst heart within
doth wither in
man's faithless hour.

DEPARTURE DAY
August 8, 2014

As quietly, my mind doth reminisce
O'er old familiar visages, remembered yet
Who once didst grace my life with vibrant life
But sadly now, doth fade into the mist
Not wilfully of course, I loved them well
Each had relationship with me to tell
In daily interchange when lips were kissed
When hand was grasped by friendly hand
Those thoughts and cares exchanged, that fell
Before the next onrush of ideas grand
That sadly are forever more, long past
As now the wheel of life doth ever turn
Inexorably, tho we seem to not discern
Until the hammer drops one fateful day
To then begin inevitable fade away
It burdens me that now I must relate
To this, the sad result of each man's fate
Where are they now, however might we tell
Wherever's that eternity where man must dwell
To mine as well, reluctant I agree
Those I now know and love will not remember me
Beyond the first few years of my demise
As I depart to God without disguise
To hide those warts and sins obtained in life
On planet earth in social interchange with men

My heavenly excursion lasts forever then
Whilst brevity of earthly stay doth fade
Those fleshly years when sin didst e'er degrade
Whilst yet I may, I bid thee fond farewell
And ask each fellow traveller to please forgive
My many sad offences whilst I yet didst live
As I forgive each sad offence from thee as well
And ere memory of me doth fade away
Think well whilst memory doth yet exist
On this unexpected, inevitable departure day

TO ENDLESS SAIL
July 25, 2014

Behold, yon stately Persian yachts,
possessors come from Camelot's
aristocratic upper class,
who suck the nations dry, alas,
to endless sail.

Behold, look to the eastern sky,
these ghostly ships go drifting by,
elusive in their majesty.
Condemned through all antiquity,
to endless sail.

Fine tendered by a ghostly crew,
in times to come, it's me, it's you?
Chained to the mast of infamy,
encumbered by our destiny,
to endless sail.

As ships endeavor out of sight
thru endless day, thru endless night.
Our chains well forged to never break,
eternal life we now forsake,
to endless sail.